Islamic Design
Workbook

Eric Broug

Islamic Design Workbook

With 48 loose-leaf activity sheets

For Andrea

Acknowledgments
My thanks go to Bashar Tabbah and Hamid Abhari
for the use of their photographs.

Picture Credits
Pages 10 (top), 12 (top), 14–15: Bashar Tabbah.
Pages 7 (bottom) and 11 (top right): Hamid Abhari.
All other photographs are by the author.

First published in the United Kingdom in 2016
by Thames & Hudson Ltd, 181A High Holborn,
London WC1V 7QX

Reprinted 2024

British Library Cataloguing-in-Publication Data
A catalogue record for this book is available from
the British Library

ISBN 978-0-500-29242-6

Printed and bound in China by Everbest Printing
Investment Ltd

Be the first to know about our new releases,
exclusive content and author events by visiting
thamesandhudson.com
thamesandhudsonusa.com
thamesandhudson.com.au

Contents

Introduction

The craftsmen and designers who created Islamic geometric patterns and compositions more than 1,000 years ago used a compass and a ruler – just as we do today – and with these two tools they drew circles and lines. By dividing a circle into equal parts, they created points of intersection along the edge of the circle. Using a ruler to connect these intersections, they formed grids of straight lines – known as construction lines – which provided the foundations for their patterns and compositions. The construction lines of the patterns featured in this book can be found on the loose-leaf sheets in the back pocket.

In Islamic geometric patterns and compositions, you cannot see all the construction lines in the finished work: some segments of the lines are used, and others are not. Deciding which segments of the lines to use determines the final pattern. This, essentially, is what this book is about: using the construction lines provided, you will be able to experiment with patterns and compositions, deciding which segments of the lines to include in your design and which to leave out. In doing so, you will be participating in a design tradition that goes back to the 7th century, encompassing the Marinid madrasas in Morocco, the Mamluk mosques in Cairo, the Timurid buildings in Samarkand and Herat, the window screens of the Umayyad Mosque in Damascus, the Great Mosque of Isfahan and the Alhambra in Granada.

Every single geometric composition in Islamic art and architecture is created in the same way, using a grid of construction lines. Islamic geometric compositions also share another characteristic: they all have the same starting point – a circle. But how do you turn a circle into a pattern? Imagine you are a craftsman in 15th-century Cairo and you have a piece of paper, a compass, a pencil and a ruler on the desk in front of you. Using your compass, you draw a circle. The next step is to create intersections along the edge of the circle, so that your

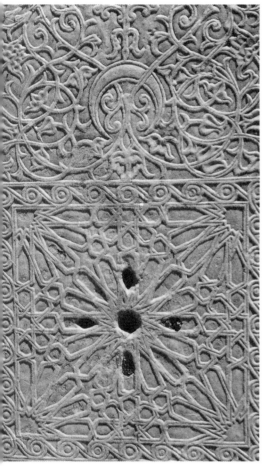

Mausoleum of Sidi Kacem Jelizi,
Tunis, Tunisia

All Islamic patterns start with a circle, which is divided into equal parts. The number of parts will determine which shapes can be created, as shown below. The resulting patterns can be as intricate as the examples above and opposite.

pattern can develop. Let's say you want to divide your circle into six equal parts. Place the point of your compass anywhere along the edge of the circle and draw a second circle of the same diameter as the first. There are two points where the circles intersect: place the point of the compass on one of these intersections and draw a third circle of the same diameter. Moving along the edge of the original circle, follow the same process: place the point of the compass on the intersection with the original circle and draw another circle, and so on, until you have six circles of the same diameter grouped around the original, central circle. Use a ruler to draw three straight lines connecting the intersections along the edge of the original circle. These lines should pass through the centre of the original circle and divide it into six equal parts. Alternatively you could choose to divide your circle into four equal parts or, with a little more knowledge and practice, ten equal parts.

These are the choices you would have faced as a 15th-century craftsman in Cairo. Most patterns fall into three main categories in Islamic geometric design – fourfold, fivefold and sixfold – each determined by the number of equal parts into which the circle that forms the basis of the composition is divided. When a circle is divided into four equal parts, the resulting pattern is known as 'fourfold'. A design based on a circle of eight, sixteen or thirty-two equal parts – i.e. multiples of four – is also fourfold. Similarly, a pattern based on a circle of six equal parts is called 'sixfold', while 'fivefold' is used to describe a pattern based on a circle of five or ten equal parts.

Around 90 per cent of all patterns and compositions in Islamic art and architecture fall into one of these three categories; the other 10 per cent includes, for example, sevenfold and elevenfold designs. Within these three main branches of the Islamic geometric design

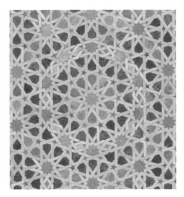

Bou Inaniya Madrasa, Fez, Morocco

Ben Youssef Madrasa,
Marrakesh, Morocco

Gunbad-i Kabud, Maragha, Iran

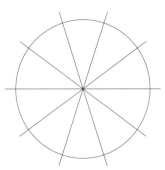

Creating a ten-pointed star pattern:

Step 1 Divide a circle into ten equal parts. Ten intersections are created along the circle's edge.

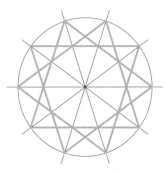

Step 2 Use a ruler to connect the intersections created in step 1, as shown above, to make a ten-pointed star.

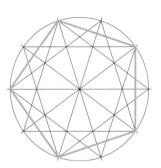

Step 3 Draw a pentagon, as highlighted, connecting five of the ten intersections created in step 1.

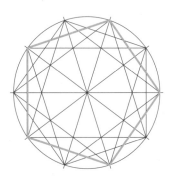

Step 4 Draw a second pentagon, connecting the remaining five intersections.

The six identical 'petal' shapes around a six-pointed star show that this pattern is based on a circle divided into six equal parts.

family tree, there is an immense variety and wealth of patterns. Each branch has its own unique characteristics. Sixfold is the biggest branch of the family and offers the most variation, with a huge number of different patterns. Fivefold is the cleverest – and most challenging – branch of the family, providing the most surprising and creative patterns and compositions. In contrast, the fourfold branch of the family is typically the most straightforward and accessible – the least problematic to read and understand.

So your first creative choice has been made: you have divided your circle into a number of equal parts. This will give you points of intersection where the straight lines meet the edge of the circle. Using a ruler, you can draw connecting lines between these intersections. You can also place the point of your compass on these intersections and draw more circles. These lines and/or circles will create more intersections, which can also be connected with lines. Lines have to be drawn in a particular order, with the resulting intersections enabling the next steps. This process can continue for several steps. Essentially new layers of construction lines are built up until you have all the lines you need for a particular pattern. Complex patterns and compositions have more of these layers. As an example, see the step-by-step guide to drawing a ten-pointed star pattern (starting top left).

Using a compass and a ruler to draw these patterns and compositions has an important benefit because it means that changing the scale of a pattern does not affect the way you draw it. Whether you are creating a large-scale pattern to adorn the full width of a mosque entrance or a much smaller design to illuminate the page of a Koran, the steps you must follow are exactly the same. For a large-scale pattern, you simply start with a large circle. It is easy to scale up or down.

It would be impossible to estimate how many different patterns and compositions have been made over the course of more than 1,000 years of design tradition. There must be hundreds, if not thousands. Many more must have been lost to history. Some patterns

The ten identical 'petal' shapes around a ten-pointed star show that this pattern is based on a circle divided into five (or ten) equal parts.

are better known than others and have been well documented in photographs and books, but these represent just a fraction of the designs through the centuries. In this book I have included some of the lesser-known patterns from across the Islamic world. By featuring them here and providing the construction lines to draw them, I hope that these neglected patterns are revived in some small way.

One of the most intriguing aspects of Islamic geometric design is the discovery of identical patterns from various periods in different parts of the world. How is it possible that craftsmen hundreds of years and thousands of kilometres apart were using the same pattern? There are a few such patterns in this book; see pages 26, 27 and 52. If we take the pattern on page 52 as an example, the caption gives the Ben Youssef Madrasa in Marrakesh as its source, but it could just as easily have come from the Alhambra in Granada, or from a fragment of ceramic wall from a Seljuk building, now in the Turkish and Islamic Arts Museum in Istanbul. One possible explanation is that knowledge was passed on from one craftsman to another, allowing these patterns to be applied in different eras and regions.

However, a more likely explanation is that craftsmen in different parts of the world, by playing around with circles, lines and intersections, worked out how to do these patterns for themselves. It seems natural that a designer of geometric patterns would have experimented with construction lines – following the first few steps of an existing composition before branching out, for example, or using the construction lines for a familiar pattern in a completely new way (see illustrations 3 and 4 on the inside flap of this book). This experimental attitude to geometric design accounts for the rich diversity of patterns across the Islamic world. It is entirely feasible that craftsmen who were in no way connected to one another came up with the same pattern. As you work on the loose-leaf sheets and become more familiar with the designs in the book, you will discover alternative compositions to draw using the same construction lines – you can be part of this design tradition of experimentation and innovation.

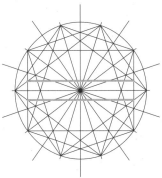

Step 5 Draw parallel lines between four of the intersections created in step 4.

Step 6 Work clockwise around the circle, drawing four more sets of parallel lines between the intersections created in step 4. The construction lines are now complete.

Step 7 Trace the segments of the construction lines that are needed to create the star pattern.

9

Mosque of Ibn Tulun, Cairo, Egypt

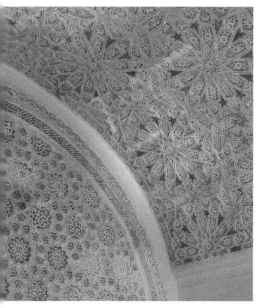

Bardo National Museum, Tunis, Tunisia

Topkapı Palace, Istanbul, Turkey

By experimenting with the patterns in this book, you will develop an understanding of Islamic geometric design. You will learn to recognize the characteristics of certain patterns. The construction lines for fourfold and fivefold patterns are markedly different, for example. This knowledge, acquired with practice, will help you to identify and deconstruct Islamic geometric patterns, making them much more accessible. You will be able to apply this knowledge whenever you see geometric works in Islamic art and architecture.

Being able to identify the geometric 'family' of a particular pattern – whether it is fourfold, fivefold, sixfold, etc – will help immensely in this process. The best way to do this is by counting the number of identical shapes arranged in a circle around a central star. Generally, the best geometric shape to count is a 'petal', as illustrated in the two diagrams at the top of pages 8 and 9. If you can count eight petal shapes, the pattern is fourfold; if you can count ten petal shapes, the pattern is fivefold, etc. It is good to get into the habit of counting the petal shapes in geometric patterns and compositions. If you count the petals in the illustrations in this book, you will soon start to recognize similarities and differences in the patterns.

The petal-shaped composition on the opposite page (which you can also draw; see page 23) is especially interesting for two reasons. First, it contains smaller-scale compositions within it, in which the petal motif is repeated. You can imagine zooming in on the petal motif ad infinitum: each petal contains its own composition, which contains petals that contain their own composition, and so on. Second, you can also imagine the petal motif as part of a larger composition with other identical petals. Instead of zooming in, you could zoom out (infinitely). This particular petal-shaped composition embodies a principle of Islamic geometric design called self-similarity. This principle also occurs in mathematics, specifically with fractals. In Islamic geometric design, self-similarity is particularly prominent in Iranian architecture. We can see that this pattern is fivefold: the central ten-pointed star is surrounded by ten identical kite shapes and ten pentagons. As the pattern in the petal is fivefold, it follows that the petal itself is also fivefold. The composition on page 28 is part of this same tradition.

Islamic geometric design offers plenty of opportunities for creative exploration. The drawings in this book are rooted in geometry and require accuracy to construct, but the visual impact of a design has always been more important than absolute precision. Close analysis of compositions in Islamic art and architecture has shown that there are many works in which craftsmen made slight adjustments for the benefit of the overall design. Typically, this happened when a composition combined patterns from different branches of the geometric family tree. The composition on page 62, from the Alhambra, combines fourfold and fivefold patterns: a central ten-pointed star is surrounded by fourfold patterns in the corners, and above and below. As a composition it is very effective. However, if

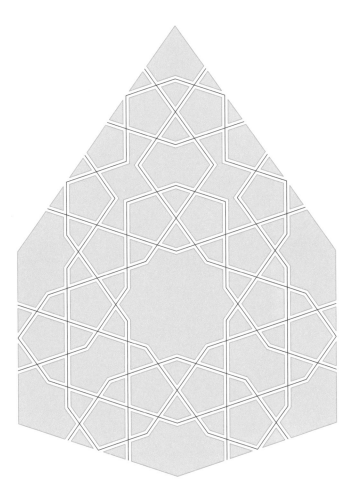

you try to draw it yourself, you will see that the designer has had to tweak the construction lines to get them to join up. Another example, on page 63, combines fourfold (in blue) and sixfold (in red) patterns. Analysis shows that the designer had to modify the six-pointed stars to make them fit. Some geometric compositions that are considered masterpieces of design have been adjusted in a similar way for visual effect. The triangular illustration on page 13, showing the main side panel from the minbar of the funerary complex of Sultan Al-Ghuri in Cairo, is a good example. The only way the designer could achieve this sophisticated composition, which combines eighteen-pointed stars with twelve- and seven-pointed stars, was by tweaking some of the construction lines. These compositions are a useful reminder that Islamic geometric design is first and foremost a form of artistic expression; there has always been creative licence to experiment and innovate.

Most of the drawings in this book could cover a limitless surface area if the pattern were repeated over and over again. This is the principle of almost all geometric patterns. The practical challenge lies in working out how the pattern can be made to repeat. Is there a rectangular or square unit (which can be the entire pattern or just part of it) that, if repeated, would join seamlessly with other identical units to form a larger composition? Some of the drawings in this book could be repeated ad infinitum. The illustration at the top of page 13 is one example: the pattern here can stand on its own as a composition (there is an exceptional page in a Mamluk Koran that does just that)

ABOVE LEFT A petal-shaped pattern showing an important principle of Islamic geometric design: self-similarity. A simple motif in a composition can contain similar, smaller-scale motifs, which in turn can contain even smaller motifs – and so on, seemingly ad infinitum. The principle of self-similarity in Islamic geometric design invites you to contemplate infinity.

ABOVE RIGHT
Gunbad-i Kabud, Maragha, Iran

Kerak Castle, Jordan

Sabil-Kuttab of Sultan Qaytbay,
Cairo, Egypt

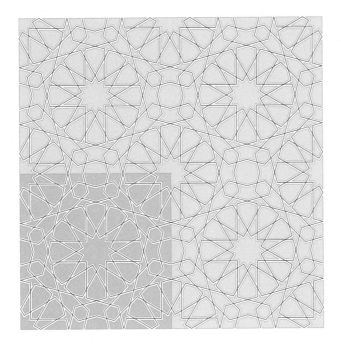

but can also be repeated as a unit in a tessellated arrangement. Any drawing in the book that has quarter stars in the corners and/or half stars along the sides can be used in this way. This is how craftsmen have designed and planned their compositions for centuries.

The best way to learn about Islamic geometric design is to try it out for yourself. By drawing patterns, you will come across the same challenges and insights that craftsmen over the centuries have experienced. You will learn to appreciate the creativity that lies behind each design as much more than simply recreating a pattern. Through trial and error, you will discover the value of taking the time to understand a pattern and using a structured approach in its execution. The construction lines on the loose-leaf sheets allow you to see the geometric foundations of patterns and compositions. They will also reward you, every now and then, by revealing the harmony of geometry and symmetry.

Kasbah of Telouet, Morocco

Patterns

1 | Tilla Kari Madrasa, Samarkand, Uzbekistan (1646–60)
The madrasa was the last and largest addition to Samarkand's famous Registan
Square. Although originally built as a madrasa, due to its large prayer hall it soon
became Samarkand's congregational mosque. Tilla Kari means 'gold-covered',
referring to the lavish decoration of its domed chamber.

2 | Jahangiri Mahal, Agra, India (1560–70)
The rooms of Jahangiri Mahal in the Agra Fort complex were constructed
to ensure maximum privacy. Built by Akbar the Great as a *zenana*,
a residential palace for the women of the Mughal court, it is one
of the few buildings from his reign to have survived intact.

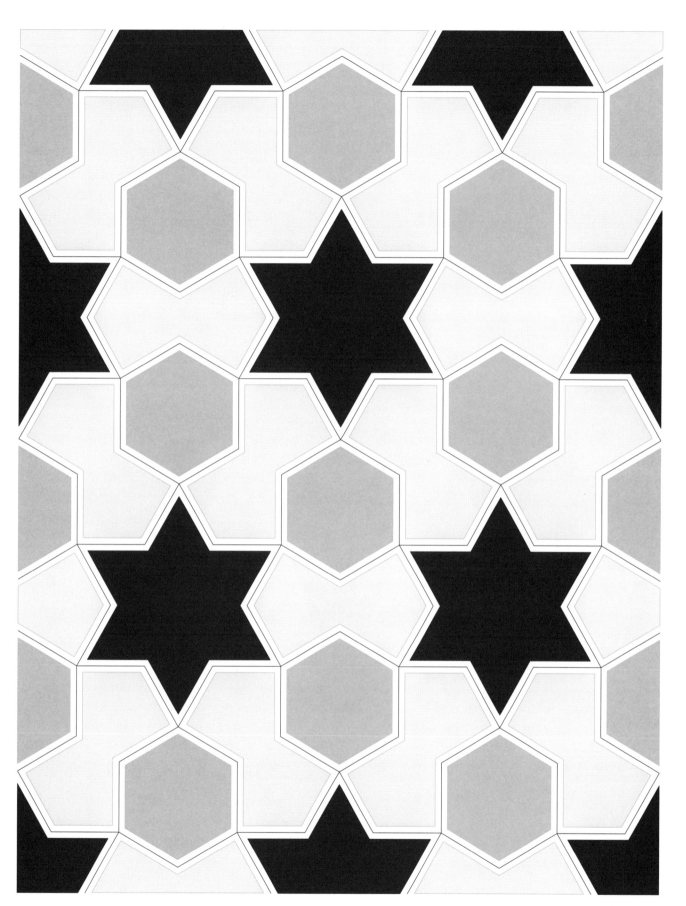

3 | Friday Mosque (Jameh Mosque), Isfahan, Iran

Built by the Seljuks when they established their capital in Isfahan in 1051, the mosque is located
on the site of a previous Buyid mosque. The building has been altered and expanded over the
centuries: the double-storey arcade was added in 1447. The mihrab of the Ilkhanid ruler Oljeitu,
considered a masterpiece of design and stucco workmanship, is found here.

4 | Humayun's Tomb, Delhi, India (1560–70)
This was the first tomb to mark the grave of a Mughal emperor, and its monumental scale became
typical of imperial Mughal architecture. It is set in a traditional garden, walled on three sides; the other
side faces what was once the Jamuna River. The tomb was designed by a Persian architect, but the
Hindu dome pavilions (*chhatris*) around the central dome show the influence of local architecture.

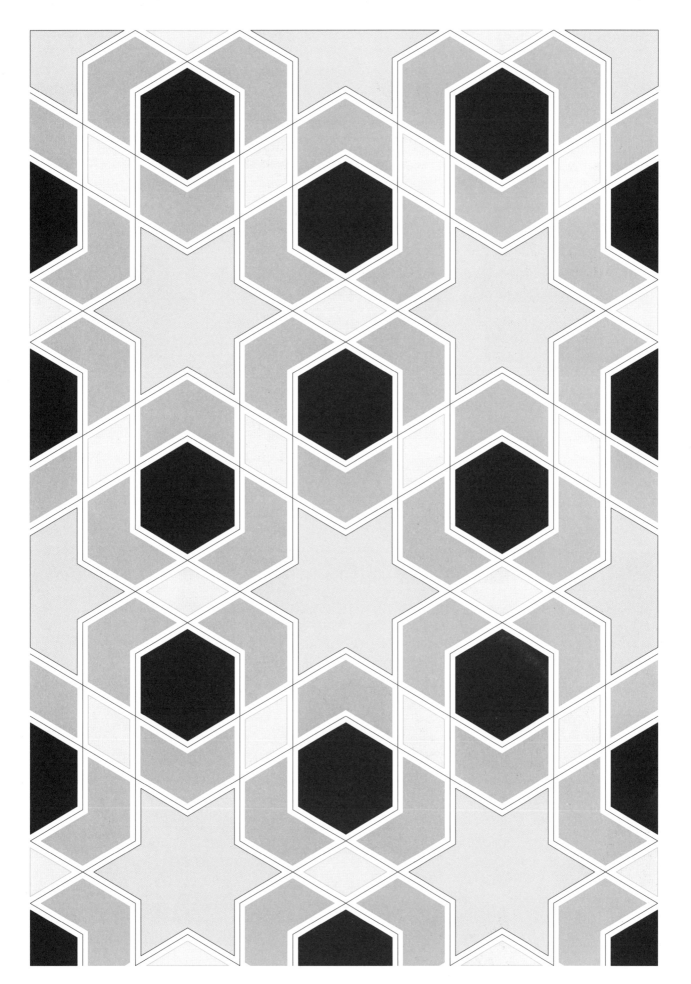

5 | Friday Mosque (Jameh Mosque) of Varzaneh, Iran (c. 1100)
Originally dating from the early 12th century, this mosque was largely rebuilt during
the Timurid era. The tilework on the arched entrance to the prayer area mentions
Shah Rukh, the youngest son of Timur – the founder of the Timurid dynasty.

6 | Mausoleum of I'timad-ud-Daulah, Agra, India (1622–28)
I'timad-ud-Daulah was the grandfather of Mumtaz Mahal, in whose honour Mughal emperor
Shah Jahan built the Taj Mahal. The mausoleum was the first Mughal building to be entirely
encased in marble. All the geometric patterns are made in pietra dura, the inlay
technique that was later used in elaborate fashion for the Taj Mahal.

7 | Petal

Petals are one of the most common shapes in Islamic geometric design and typically appear grouped
around a central star pattern. Counting how many petals appear around a star is a quick and easy
way to determine the category of the pattern – whether it is fourfold, fivefold or sixfold, etc.
The composition above is an example of a self-similar geometric pattern (see page 10).

8 | Amer Fort, Jaipur, India (1592)
One of Rajasthan's most famous forts, Amer Fort was the residence of the Rajput maharajas.
Also known as Amer Palace, it is laid out on four levels, each with its own courtyard.
Built in red sandstone and marble, it overlooks a lake and has an imposing presence,
set high on a hill with various ramparts leading up to its gates.

9 | Tomb of Akbar the Great, Agra, India (1605–13)
Construction of the tomb began in Akbar's lifetime. Much like the tomb of his father,
Humayun, this tomb is set in the centre of a large walled garden, divided into quadrants.
It is constructed mainly in red sandstone, combined with white marble, and is adorned
with many geometric compositions.

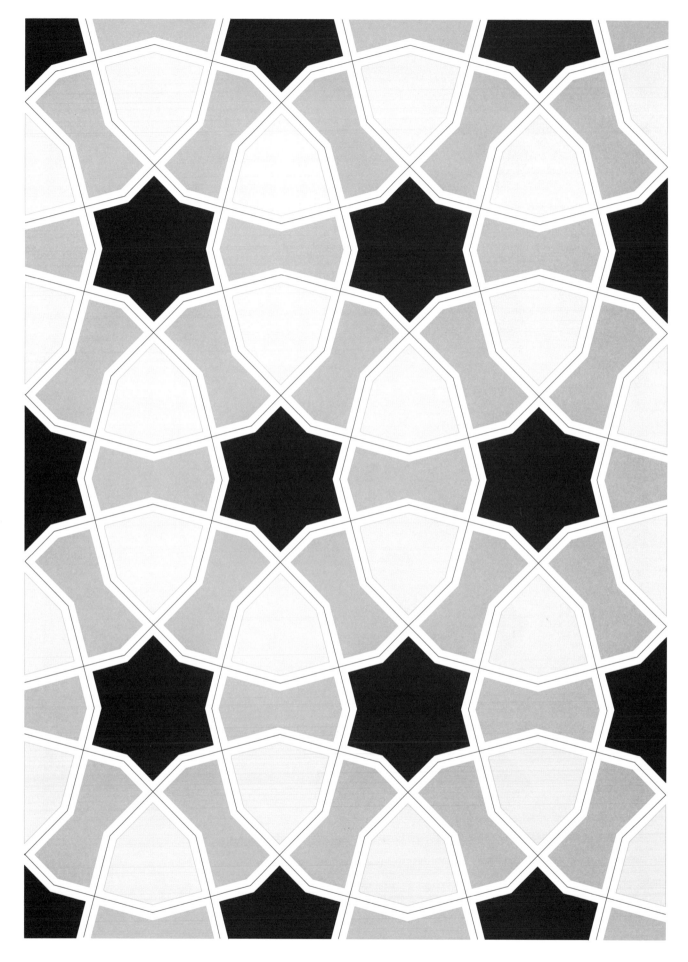

10 | Shah-i Zinda, Samarkand, Uzbekistan (11th–15th centuries)
This group of mausolea, built between the 11th and 15th centuries, comprised more than twenty
buildings. Its name means 'the living king' and refers to the legend that Kusam ibn Abbas, cousin
of the Prophet Muhammad, was buried here. The entire complex is richly decorated with a variety
of materials, techniques and visual themes.

11 | Ulugh Beg Madrasa, Bukhara, Uzbekistan (1417–21)
Ulugh Beg was Timur's grandson and is known not only as a sultan, but also as
an astronomer and mathematician. He built an observatory in Samarkand that
was the finest and largest in the Islamic world.

12 | Pentagonal star

Pentagons are common in Islamic geometric design. Craftsmen over the centuries have typically found the greatest creative challenge and reward in fivefold patterns because they do not follow the same rules as fourfold and sixfold patterns. This particular pentagon contains a ten-pointed star pattern and, like the composition on page 23, is self-similar.

13 | Kukeldash Madrasa, Bukhara, Uzbekistan (1568–69)
This madrasa, one of the largest in Central Asia, was built by an emir who held the
highly influential post of *kukeldash* (foster brother) to several khans of the Shaibanid
dynasty. It was the first structure built as part of the Lyabi Khauz complex, a group
of monumental buildings arranged around a traditional pond in Bukhara.

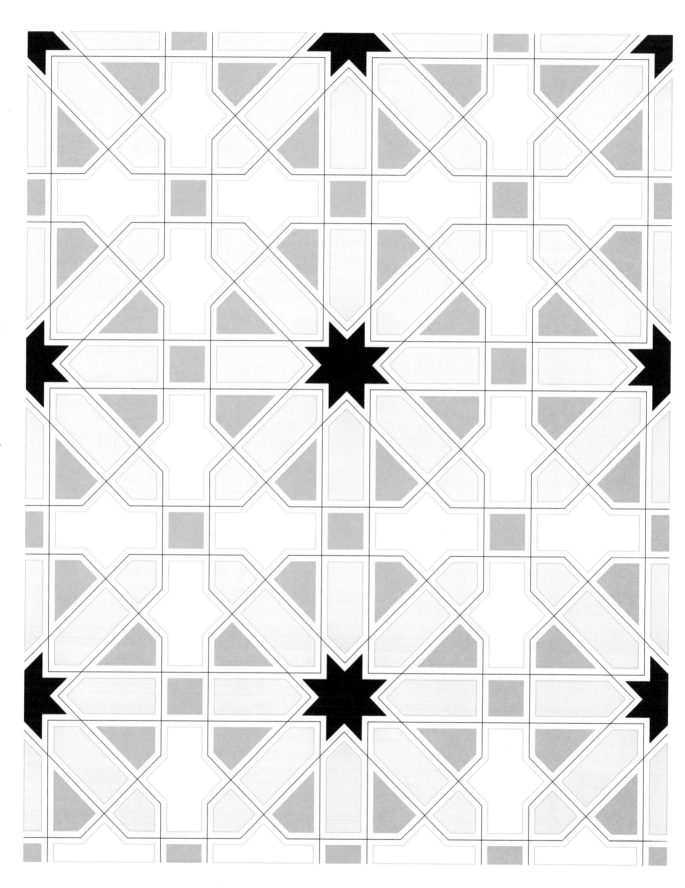

14 | Tomb of Salim Chisti, Fatehpur Sikri, India (1571–80)
The tomb is located inside the complex of the Friday Mosque. Salim Chisti was a Sufi
saint who advised Akbar the Great. To show his gratitude, Akbar named his firstborn
son – later known as the emperor Jahangir – after him. The tomb is a pilgrimage
destination for Muslims and Hindus.

15 | Friday Mosque (Jama Masjid) of Herat, Afghanistan (1200–1)
Built by the Ghurids on the site of two earlier mosques, the building fell into ruin when
Genghis Khan pillaged the province. Over the centuries, it has been rebuilt and altered.
The Ghurids were also responsible for the remarkable 62-m (203-ft) Minaret of Jam, which
is built entirely of bricks and is covered in geometric patterns and calligraphic verse.

16 | Gunbad-i Kabud, Maragha, Iran (1196–97)
Part of a group of three tomb towers, this elaborately decorated decagonal structure is covered
in sophisticated fivefold patterns that have fascinated mathematicians for centuries. Maragha
was once home to one of the world's most prestigious observatories, established in 1259.

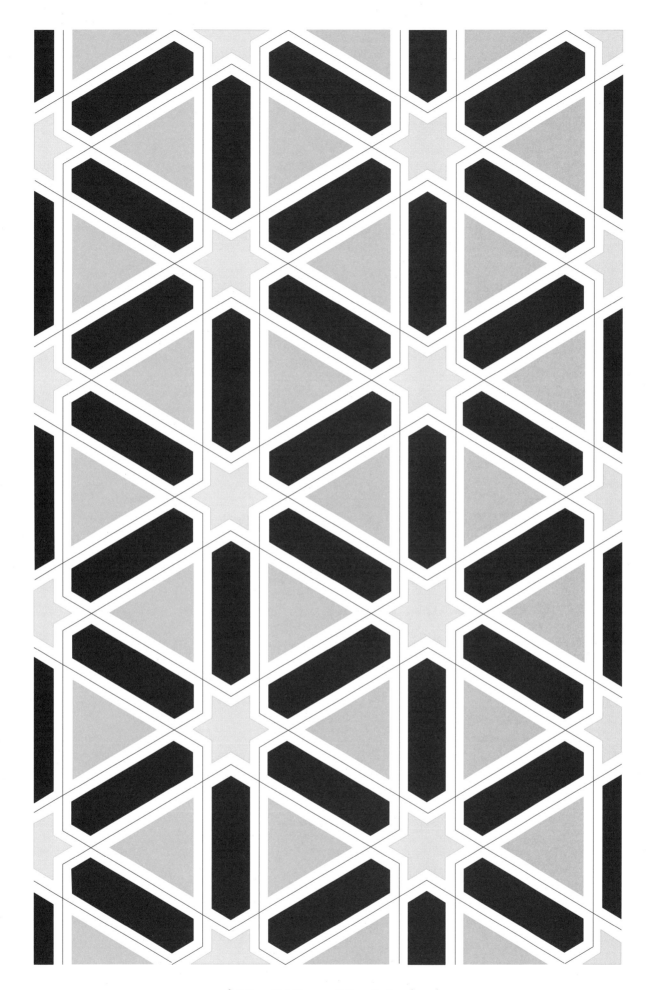

1 | Edirne Old Mosque, Edirne, Turkey (1414)
Also known as the Eski Camii, it was originally built as a Friday Mosque and became
the 'Old Mosque' when Uc Serefeli Mosque was completed in 1447. Edirne served
as the capital of the Ottoman Empire between 1363 and 1453.

2 | Ince Minareli Madrasa, Konya, Turkey (1264–65)
The madrasa is named after its once very tall, slender minaret, which largely collapsed
in the early 20th century. The entrance portal is elaborately decorated, with interlacing
bands of calligraphy that frame the doorway, as well as plant motifs. It now houses
the Museum of Stone and Wood Art.

3 | Mamluk Koran (c. 1306–15)
This composition is taken from a single-volume Koran by master illuminator Sandal,
although the name of the patron is not known. In this Koran, the central star bears verse
42 from the Fussilat, which was rarely used by other Koran illuminators but was
favoured by Sandal. It is now kept in the Chester Beatty Library in Dublin.

4 | Sultan Han, Sultanhani, Turkey (1229)
Sultan Han is one of the largest caravanserais in Turkey and is one of only three
in the Aksaray Province. It is located on the ancient trade route from Konya to
Persia. Sultan Han's massive stone walls and single entrance protected its
visitors and their produce.

5 | Döner Kümbet, Kayseri, Turkey (1276)
Döner Kümbet is translated as the 'rotating tomb'. Built for Princess Sah Cihan
Hatun, it is one of the most finely decorated Seljuk tombs in Kayseri. The tomb
is covered in plant and animal motifs, as well as geometric patterns.

6 | Ak Madrasa, Nigde, Turkey (1404)
Built by the Karamanids in local sandstone, the *pishtaq* (entrance portico)
is particularly richly decorated with geometric and floral motifs, and topped
by an elaborate *muqarnas* (vaulting).

7 | Complex of Sultan Murad II, Bursa, Turkey (1426–28)
Also known as the Muradiye, the complex consists of a mosque, madrasa, *imaret* (soup kitchen)
and twelve mausolea (*türbe*) belonging to the sultan's family. Murad II was the last
Ottoman sultan to reign from the original Ottoman capital of Bursa.

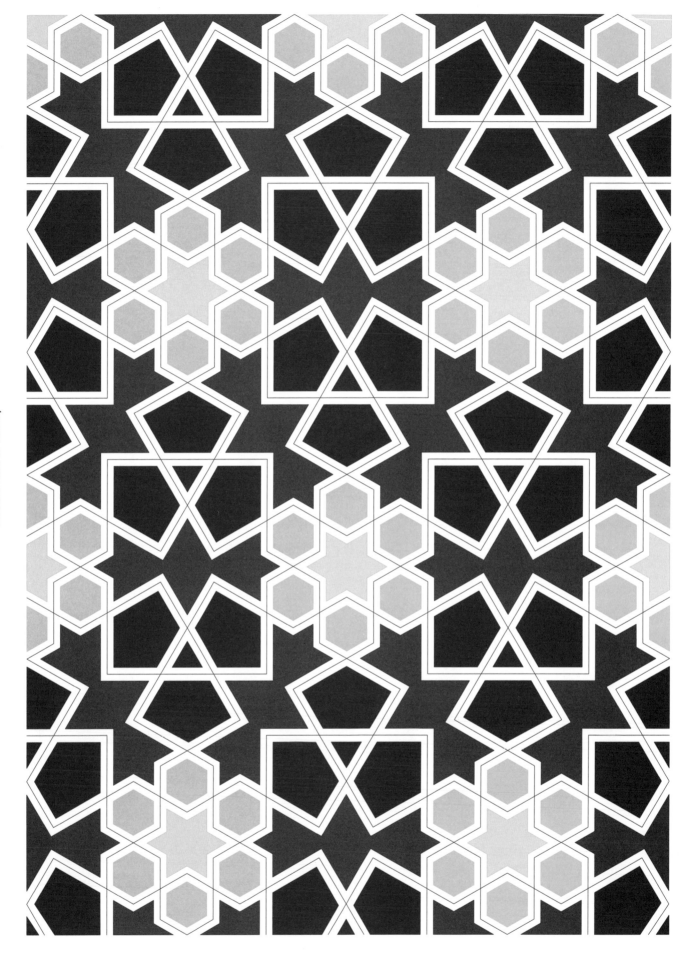

8 | Wooden mihrab from the shrine of Sayyida Ruqayya, Cairo, Egypt (1133)
Made by order of the wife of the reigning Fatimid caliph, the mihrab is decorated
on all sides, suggesting that it was intended as a freestanding structure.
Sayyida Ruqayya was related to the Prophet Muhammad by marriage.

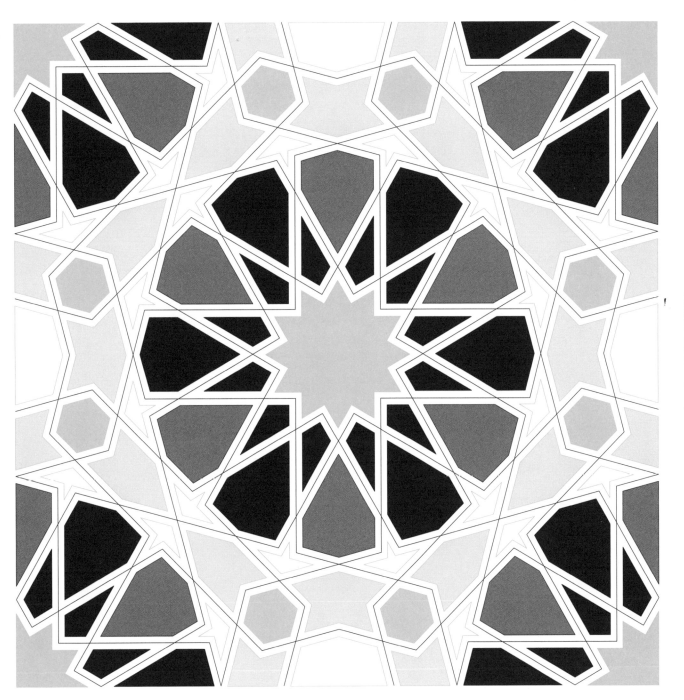

9 | Umayyad Mosque, Damascus, Syria (709–15)

The first monumental work of architecture in Islamic history, the mosque was built during
the reign of caliph Al-Walid ibn Abd al-Malik, who proclaimed: 'Inhabitants of Damascus,
four things give you marked superiority over the rest of the world: your climate, your water,
your fruits and your baths. To these I wanted to add a fifth: this mosque.'

10 | Al-Azhar Mosque, Cairo, Egypt (founded in 970)
Commissioned in 970 by Fatimid caliph Al-Mu'izz li-Din Allah, this was the first
mosque to be established in Cairo. Al-Azhar University was established later, in 988.
Over the centuries, the mosque has undergone many alterations.

11 | Door of the *imaret* (soup kitchen) of Ibrahim Bey of Konya, Karaman, Turkey (1451)
The *imaret* is part of a complex that includes a mosque, a madrasa and a mausoleum
and is one of the best examples of Karamanid architecture. The door is now in the Turkish
and Islamic Arts Museum in Istanbul.

12 | Al-Mustansiriya Madrasa, Baghdad, Iraq (1227–34)
Established by Abbasid caliph Al-Mustansir, the madrasa had a huge library and was
the first to unify the four orthodox Sunni schools of law, Hanbali, Shafii, Maliki and
Hanaf. Each school occupied a corner of the madrasa.

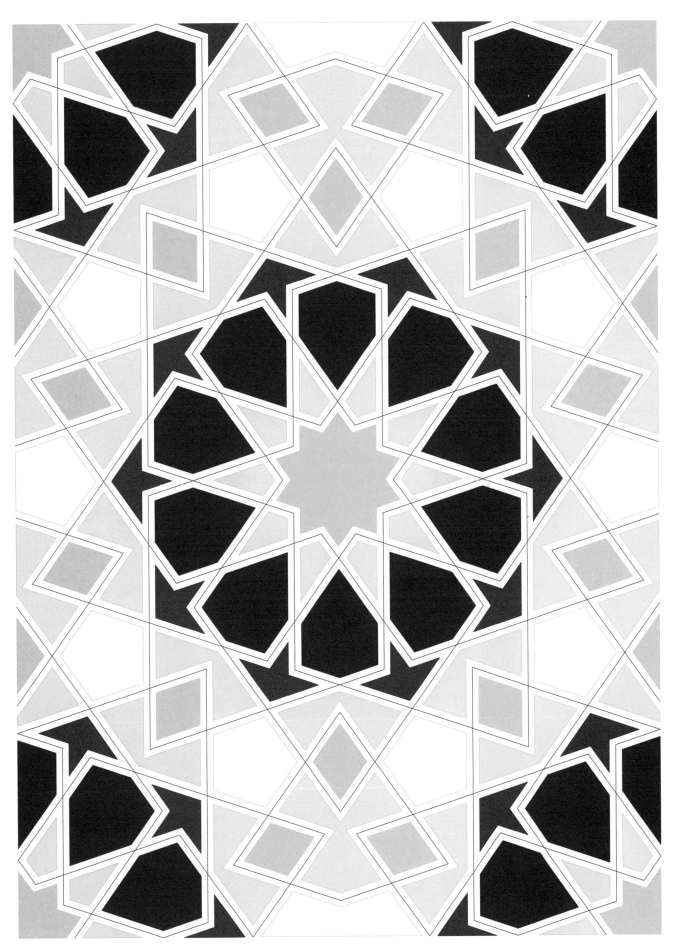

13 | Koran box of Selim II (died 1574)
Standing 164 cm (65 in.) high, this Koran box is considered to be a masterpiece
of Ottoman design and inlay. This drawing shows one panel of the Koran box.
The geometric composition is made in mother-of-pearl inlay. It is now in the Turkish
and Islamic Arts Museum in Istanbul.

14 | The Aqsunqur Mosque, Cairo, Egypt (1346–47)
Emir Aqsunqur is said to have personally supervised the construction of the mosque.
It is not typical of the Mamluk mosques of the period and bears similarities to the
Great Mosque of Tripoli, where Aqsunqur was governor before he moved to Cairo.

15 | Al-Mustansiriya Madrasa, Baghdad, Iraq (1227–34)
Considered one of the oldest centres of learning, the madrasa attracted students from
across the Islamic world. They came to study theology, literature, medicine, mathematics,
jurisprudence and the Koran. The brick façades of the madrasa feature dozens of
geometric compositions.

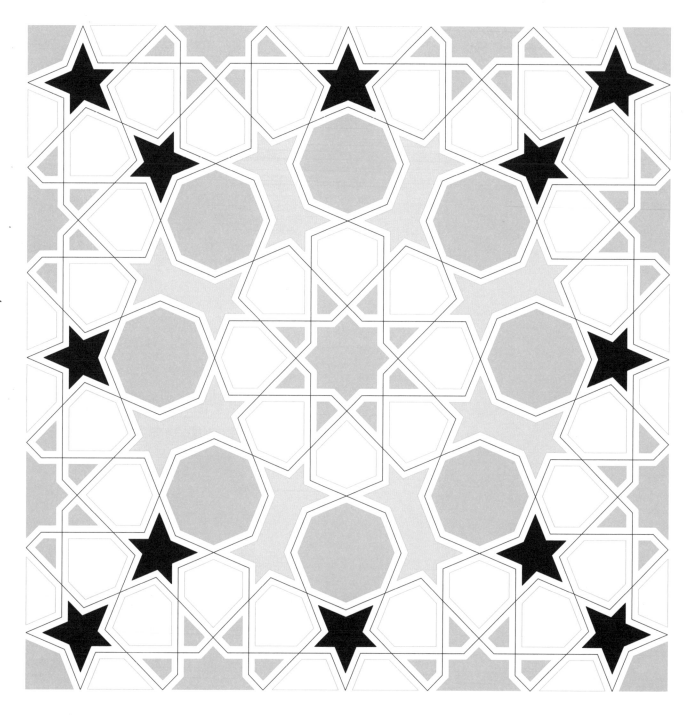

16 | Sultan Lajin's Minbar at the Mosque of Ibn Tulun, Cairo, Egypt (1296)
Before he became sultan, Hussam al-Din Lajin spent a year in hiding in the Mosque of Ibn Tulun
due to his complicity in an assassination. He vowed to restore the mosque if he survived.
When he became sultan, he kept his word and had the minbar built.

1 | Sultan's Palace, Tangier, Morocco (1684)
Also known as Dar al-Makhzen, the palace was built during the reign of Sultan Moulay Ismail.
The last sultan of independent Morocco was exiled here in 1912 when he was forced to
abdicate by the French Protectorate. He moved his entire court to the palace.

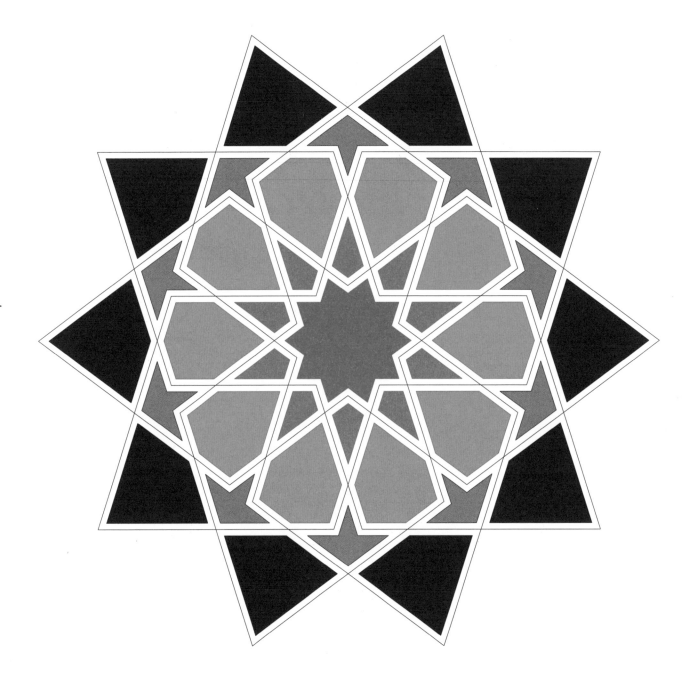

2 | Bou Inaniya Madrasa, Fez, Morocco (1355)
The Marinids built many beautiful madrasas in Morocco, and the Bou Inaniya Madrasa is perhaps
the most celebrated. It was an educational institute as well as a mosque, and had shops along its
façade. The elaborate decorative style shows how the Marinids were influenced by the decoration
of the Alhambra Palace of the Nasrids in Granada, Spain.

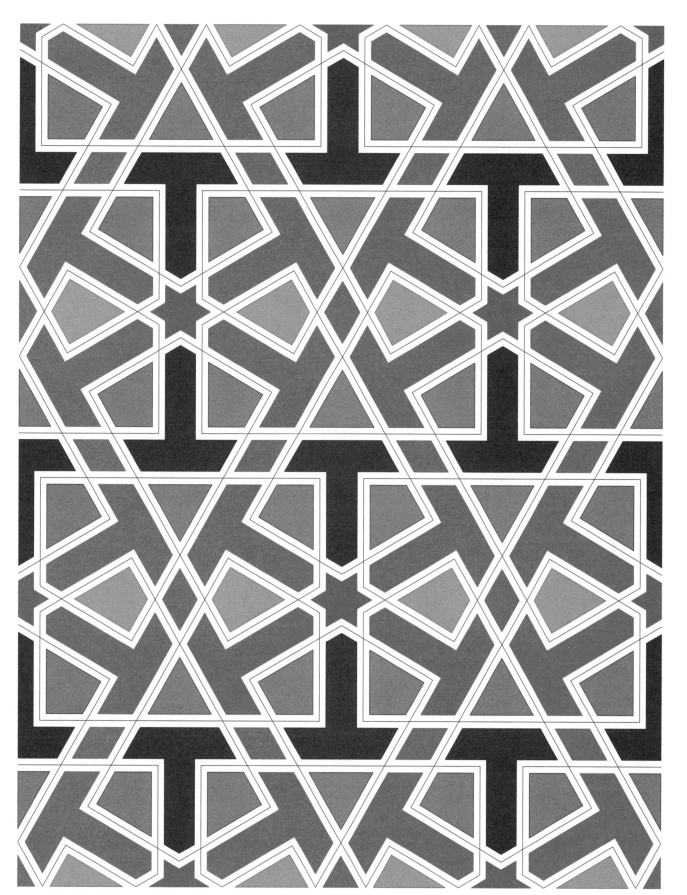

3 | Alcázar, Seville, Spain (1364)
Originally constructed as an Almohad palace on the site of a 10th-century fort, the
Alcázar was largely rebuilt in 1364 for the Christian ruler Pedro I. It is considered one
of the best examples of Mudejar craftsmanship. Mudejar is the term used for Muslims
who stayed in Andalusia after it was reconquered by the Christian kings.

4 | Ben Youssef Madrasa, Marrakesh, Morocco (1564–65)
One of the few Moroccan madrasas not to have been built by the Marinids,
Ben Youssef is named after a Wattasid ruler and was built by a Saadi sultan
after the fall of the Marinid dynasty. The walls around the central courtyard
are decorated with numerous geometric compositions.

5 | Dar al-Makhzen, Rabat, Morocco (1864)
The official residence of the king of Morocco, this royal palace was built by
French architects and has extensive formal gardens. It boasts several pairs
of substantial brass doors at its main entrance, decorated with striking,
skilfully executed geometric designs.

6 | Octagonal wooden ceiling design, Marrakesh, Morocco
Craftsmen in Morocco have a tradition of making very large and detailed
wooden ceilings, typically in an octagonal frame. Octagonal ceilings are
common in Islamic architecture because they are a transitional step between
a space with four walls and the dome above.

7 | Moroccan wooden ceiling
Moroccan craftsmen use this particular design frequently when making
large wooden ceilings. They typically use a full-size template that consists
of a triangular wedge representing one sixteenth of the ceiling. This is all
they need to make the entire ceiling.

8 | Saffarin Madrasa, Fez, Morocco (1271)
Its name means the 'madrasa of the metalworkers'. Like other Marinid madrasas,
it is richly decorated, although its student accommodation is unadorned. Its decorative
theme is clearly inspired by the Alhambra Palace of the Nasrids in Granada, Spain.

9 | Kasbah of Telouet, Morocco (1860s)

Located in the Atlas Mountains, this is one of several kasbahs along the ancient trading
route between the Sahara and Marrakesh. Built by the Glaoui family in the 19th century,
it fell to ruin when the family was exiled after Moroccan independence in 1956.

10 | Attarine Madrasa, Fez, Morocco (1323–25)
The name of this madrasa comes from its location: it is near the souk El-Attarine, the spice and
perfume market. Like other Marinid madrasas, it is richly decorated with geometric glazed tiles,
stucco carvings and calligraphy. There are thirty rooms, which could house sixty students. The
celebrated 14th-century Moroccan mathematician and astronomer Ibn al-Banna taught here.

11 | Saadian Tombs, Marrakesh, Morocco
Located in a walled garden, the tombs served as the burial site for the Saadian
sharifs of Morocco between 1557 and 1565. The gardens are accessible through a
single, narrow corridor. The two mausolea in the garden are elaborately decorated
with geometric glazed tiles.

12 | Chella Necropolis, Rabat, Morocco (1310–39)
Located just outside Rabat, this site houses the tombs of several Marinid rulers. It was built
on the ruins of a Roman harbour city, which in turn stood on the site of a Phoenician
or Carthaginian settlement known as Chella, dating from the 3rd century BC. Although
the site is now largely in ruins, architectural details evoke its former grandeur.

13 | Great Mosque of Córdoba, Spain (784–86)

Originally the building on the site was a church. After the Muslim conquest of Andalusia
in 711, the church was divided into Christian and Muslim halves. This arrangement lasted
until 784 when a mosque was built on the site. Córdoba returned to Christian rule in
1236 and the mosque was converted to a cathedral.

14 | Alhambra, Granada, Spain (1302–91)
Founded by Muhammad I, the first Nasrid sultan, in the 13th century, and substantially enlarged
and embellished by his successors, the walled Alhambra complex comprised a fortress, baths, mosques,
palaces, gardens and industrial sites. It has remained relatively intact since the 14th century and is a
valuable source of information about Islamic palatial architecture and Nasrid-style geometric design.

15 | Monastery of La Mejorada, Valladolid, Spain (1409)

Once occupied by the Order of San Geronimo, the monastery has a famous Mudejar chapel,
which has been a national monument since 1931. The Mudejar style of architecture and
decoration is strongly influenced by Moorish tastes and craftsmanship.

16 | Mexuar Hall, Alhambra, Granada, Spain (1314–59)
This was a formal hall where the sultan had meetings with his council of ministers.
It also served as a waiting room as the sultan dispensed justice. It has been altered
many times over the centuries. Mexuar Hall has an intricately detailed mihrab,
with a horseshoe-shaped arch.

1 | Tilla Kari Madrasa, Samarkand, Uzbekistan (1646–60)

Iran, Central & South Asia

2 | Jahangiri Mahal, Agra, India (1560–70)

Iran, Central & South Asia

3 | Friday Mosque (Jameh Mosque), Isfahan, Iran

Iran, Central & South Asia

4 | Humayun's Tomb, Delhi, India (1560–70)

5 | Friday Mosque (Jameh Mosque) of Varzaneh, Iran (c. 1100)

Iran, Central & South Asia

6 | Mausoleum of I'timad-ud-Daulah, Agra, India (1622–28)

7 | Petal

Iran, Central & South Asia

9 | **Tomb of Akbar the Great, Agra, India (1605–13)**

Iran, Central & South Asia

10 | Shah-i Zinda, Samarkand, Uzbekistan (11th–15th centuries)

Iran, Central & South Asia

11 | Ulugh Beg Madrasa, Bukhara, Uzbekistan (1417–21)

Iran, Central & South Asia

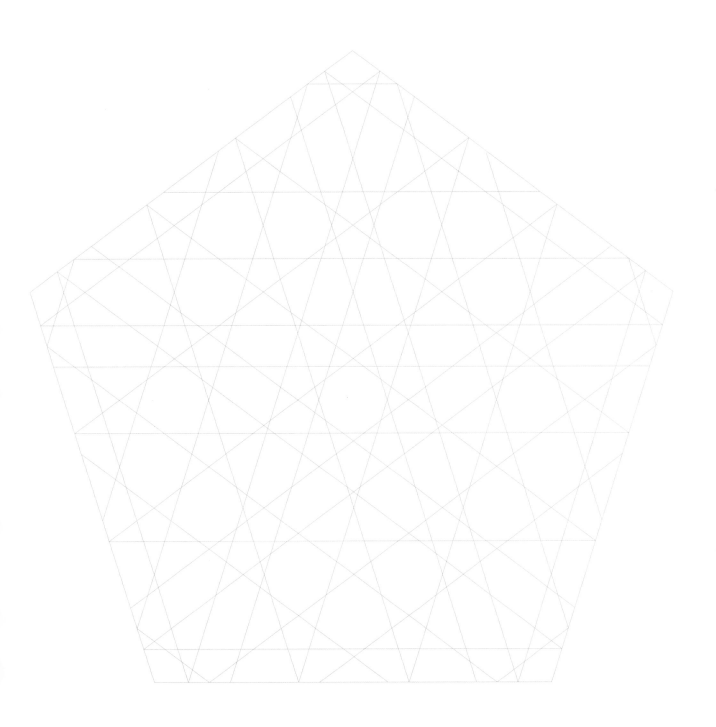

13 | Kukeldash Madrasa, Bukhara, Uzbekistan (1568–69)

Iran, Central & South Asia

14 | Tomb of Salim Chisti, Fatehpur Sikri, India (1571–80)

15 | Friday Mosque (Jama Masjid) of Herat, Afghanistan (1200–1)

Iran, Central & South Asia

16 | Gunbad-i Kabud, Maragha, Iran (1196–97)

1 | Edirne Old Mosque, Edirne, Turkey (1414)

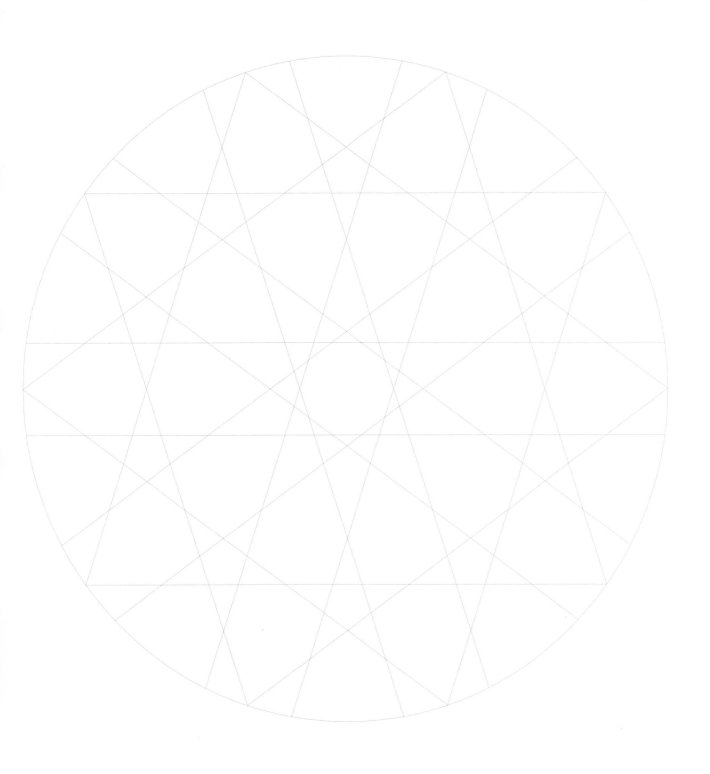

2 | Ince Minareli Madrasa, Konya, Turkey (1264–65)

3 | Mamluk Koran (c. 1306–15)

Middle East & Turkey

4 | Sultan Han, Sultanhani, Turkey (1229)

5 | Döner Kümbet, Kayseri, Turkey (1276)

Middle East & Turkey

6 | Ak Madrasa, Nigde, Turkey (1404)

8 | Wooden mihrab from the shrine of Sayyida Ruqayya, Cairo, Egypt (1133)

9 | Umayyad Mosque, Damascus, Syria (709–15)

10 | Al-Azhar Mosque, Cairo, Egypt (founded in 970)

11 | Door of the *imaret* (soup kitchen) of Ibrahim Bey of Konya, Karaman, Turkey (1451)

Middle East & Turkey

12 | Al-Mustansiriya Madrasa, Baghdad, Iraq (1227–34)

13 | Koran box of Selim II (died 1574)

Middle East & Turkey

14 | The Aqsunqur Mosque, Cairo, Egypt (1346–47)

Middle East & Turkey

15 | Al-Mustansiriya Madrasa, Baghdad, Iraq (1227–34)

1 | Sultan's Palace, Tangier, Morocco (1684)

North Africa & Spain

2 | Bou Inaniya Madrasa, Fez, Morocco (1355)

North Africa & Spain

3 | Alcázar, Seville, Spain (1364)

North Africa & Spain

4 | Ben Youssef Madrasa, Marrakesh, Morocco (1564–65)

North Africa & Spain

5 | Dar al-Makhzen, Rabat, Morocco (1864)

North Africa & Spain

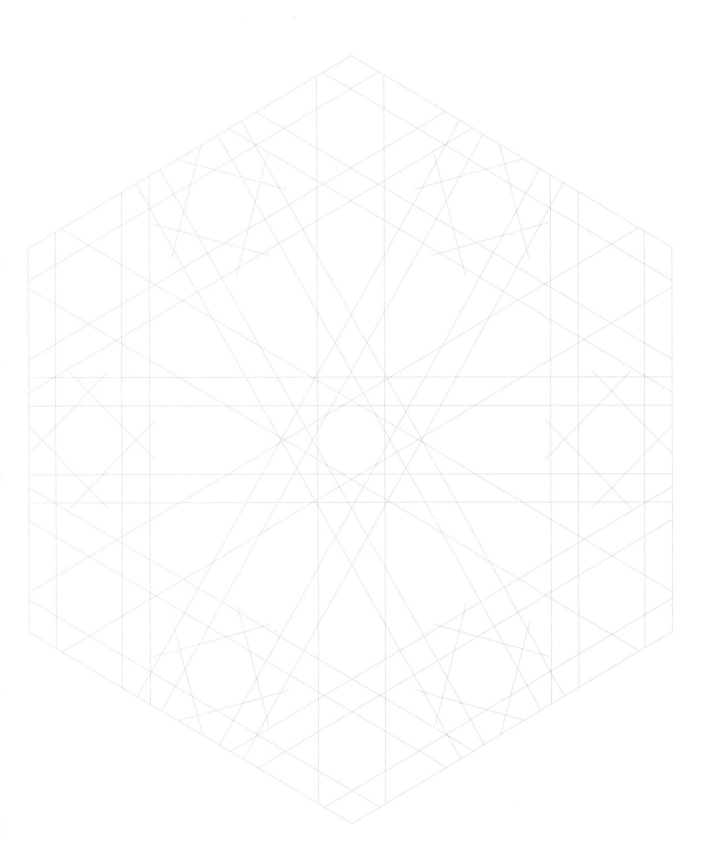

6 | Octagonal wooden ceiling design, Marrakesh, Morocco

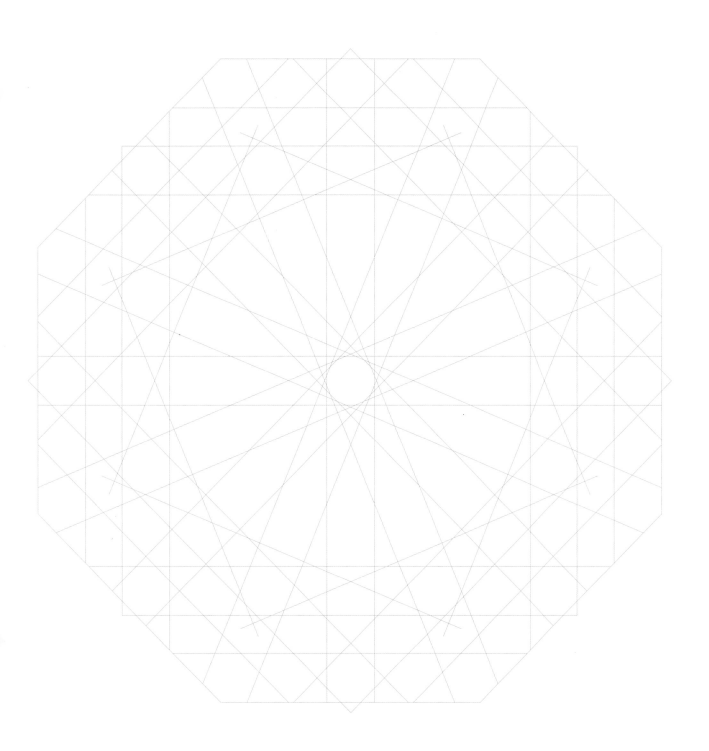

8 | Saffarin Madrasa, Fez, Morocco (1271)

9 | Kasbah of Telouet, Morocco (1860s)

North Africa & Spain

10 | Attarine Madrasa, Fez, Morocco (1323–25)

North Africa & Spain

11 | Saadian Tombs, Marrakesh, Morocco

North Africa & Spain

13 | Great Mosque of Córdoba, Spain (784–86)

14 | Alhambra, Granada, Spain (1302–91)

North Africa & Spain

15 | Monastery of La Mejorada, Valladolid, Spain (1409)

16 | Mexuar Hall, Alhambra, Granada, Spain (1314–59)